P9-APS-031

Contents at a Glance

Part I   **Welcome to WebObjects**

Chapter 1   **WebObjects and OpenBase**   3
Chapter 2   **The World of Application Servers**   13
Chapter 3   **Object-Oriented Programming**   31
Chapter 4   **Databases Today**   45

Part II   **Building a Database with OpenBase**

Chapter 5   **Creating and Using a Database**   65
Chapter 6   **Using SQL**   89
Chapter 7   **Running and Maintaining the Database**   103

Part III   **Interacting with Databases Using Enterprise Objects**

Chapter 8   **Introduction to Enterprise Objects Framework**   119
Chapter 9   **Enterprise Objects Framework Design Issues**   129
Chapter 10   **Persistent Objects**   147
Chapter 11   **Using EOModeler**   161
Chapter 12   **Working with the Model and the Database**   179

Part IV   **Creating Dynamic Web Sites with WebObjects**

Chapter 13   **WebObjects at Work**   193

Chapter 14   **Using WebObjects Builder** **215**

Chapter 15   **Using Project Builder** **229**

Chapter 16   **Using Dynamic Elements** **243**

Chapter 17   **Implementing the Request-Response Loop** **271**

Chapter 18   **Using Direct and Component Actions** **281**

Chapter 19   **State and Session Management** **293**

Chapter 20   **XML and WebObjects** **315**

Chapter 21   **Advanced WebObjects Topics** **335**

Part V   **Jump-Starting WebObjects and OpenBase**

Chapter 22   **Direct to Web** **347**

Chapter 23   **Java Client** **369**

Chapter 24   **Reusable Components in WebObjects** **387**

Chapter 25   **Reusable Databases and Frameworks in OpenBase and WebObjects** . . .   **403**

Part VI   **Deployment Issues**

Chapter 26   **Running a Database on a Network** **415**

Chapter 27   **Security** **425**

Chapter 28   **Deploying WebObjects Applications** **441**

Index **457**

Contents

Acknowledgments . . . . *xvii*

Preface . . . . *xix*

Part I	**Welcome to WebObjects**	

Chapter 1	**WebObjects and OpenBase**	**3**
	WebObjects History	4
	WebObjects: The Big Picture	7
	WebObjects: The Details	8
	Enterprise Objects Framework	8
	Development Tools	8
	Deployment Tools	9
	Production Environments	9
	Development Environments	10
	Database Environments	10
	OpenBase	10
	Before You Start: Two Cautions	11

Chapter 2	**The World of Application Servers**	**13**
	Internet and Web Basics	14
	The Importance of Standards	15
	TCP/IP	16
	HTTP	17
	HTTP and Web Servers	19
	HTML	20
	LDAP	23
	Multi-Tier Application Design	23
	Primordial Ooze	23
	The Rise of Transaction Processing Operating Systems	24
	Client/Server	25
	Three-Tier Architecture	27
	Multi-tier Architecture	28

Chapter 3	**Object-Oriented Programming**	**31**
	Object-Oriented Programming Defined	32

Object-Oriented Programming Terms and Concepts 33

Encapsulation and Accessor Methods 34

Interface Access 35

Inheritance 35

Polymorphism 36

Initialization 37

Destruction 37

Other Methods 37

Multiple Inheritance 38

Classes vs. Objects 38

Instantiation, Identification, and Location 38

Advantages of Object-Oriented Programming 39

Simplifying Code 39

Maximizing Code Reuse 40

Components and Frameworks 41

Components 41

Frameworks 43

Chapter 4 **Databases Today** **45**

Overview 46

The Database Market 46

The Roles of Databases on the Web 47

Terminology 50

What Is a Database? 50

Database Administrators 51

Data Design 51

Processing 52

Mirroring 56

Database Design 56

The Relational Model 57

Normalization 58

Aspects of Database Programming 61

SQL 61

ODBC and JDBC 61

Transactions 62

Part II **Building a Database with OpenBase**

Chapter 5 **Creating and Using a Database** **65**

The SiteDemo Database 66

What You Can Do with SiteDemo 67

SiteDemo Design 68

Working with OpenBaseManager Schema Editor 71

Building WebObjects 5 Applications

About the Author

Jesse Feiler is the author of several Mac OS X books including *Mac OS X: The Complete Reference*, *Mac OS X Developer's Guide*, and *Java Programming on Mac OS X*. He is also the author of *WebObjects 5 Developer's Guide*, as well as many books on the Web-based enterprise (such as *Database-Driven Web Sites* and *Managing the Web-Based Enterprise*), the Y2K problem, home offices, databases, and FileMaker. His books on OpenDoc, Cyberdog, Apple Guide, and Rhapsody are now collector's items.

He has worked as a developer and manager for companies such as the Federal Reserve Bank of New York (monetary policy and bank supervision), Prodigy (early Web browser), Apple Computer (information systems), New York State Department of Health (rabies and lead poisoning), The Johnson Company (office management), and Young & Rubicam (media planning and new product development).

His interest in new forms of technical training have led him to MediaSchool (http://www.mediaschool.com), for which he has authored several Mac OS X courses available over the Internet, as well as to Geek Cruises' Mac Mania cruise to Alaska. He is also the first author of a technical book to be published both on paper and on an e-book.

Active in his community, he is President of the Mid-Hudson Library System, Chair of the Philmont Comprehensive Plan Board, founder of the Philmont Main Street Committee, and Treasurer of the HB Playwrights Foundation.

He lives 100 miles north of New York City in the village of Philmont with a rescued greyhound and a cat. His research into iMovie, iDVD, and Image Capture has earned him the sobriquet "The Digital Scourge of Philmont."

Building WebObjects 5
Applications

Jesse Feiler

McGraw-Hill/Osborne

New York   Chicago   San Francisco
Lisbon   London   Madrid   Mexico City
Milan   New Delhi   San Juan
Seoul   Singapore   Sydney   Toronto

McGraw-Hill/Osborne
2600 Tenth Street
Berkeley, California 94710
U.S.A.

To arrange bulk purchase discounts for sales promotions, premiums, or fund-raisers, please contact **McGraw-Hill**/Osborne at the above address. For information on translations or book distributors outside the U.S.A., please see the International Contact Information page immediately following the index of this book.

Building WebObjects 5 Applications

1234567890 CUS CUS 01987654322

ISBN 0-07-213088-1

Publisher	Brandon A. Nordin
Vice President & Associate Publisher	Scott Rogers
Senior Acquisitions Editor	Jane Brownlow
Senior Project Editor	Carolyn Welch
Acquisitions Coordinators	Emma Acker, Ross Doll
Technical Editor	Scott Keith
Copy Editors	Chrisa Hotchkiss, Bob Campbell
Proofreader	Stefany Otis
Indexer	Jack Lewis
Computer Designers	Tabitha M. Cagan, Lucie Ericksen
Illustrators	Michael Mueller, Lyssa Wald
Series Design	Roberta Steele
Cover Series Designer	Greg Scott
Cover Illustrator	Eliot Bergman

This book was composed with Corel VENTURA™ Publisher.

Building Relationships 76

Modifying Data with OpenBase 81

Creating and Running Queries in OpenBase 83

    Default Database Queries 83

    Manipulating Results 86

    Customized Queries 86

    System Table Queries 86

Chapter 6   **Using SQL** **89**

SQL Overview 90

Retrieving Data with SELECT Statements 92

    Combining and Manipulating Columns 93

    Combining Tables Using Joins 93

    Specifying Retrieval Conditions with Where Clauses 95

Subqueries 96

Adding Data to the Database 97

Updating Data 98

Deleting Data 98

SQL Functions 98

Creating and Altering Tables 99

Creating Views 100

Using Indexes 100

Chapter 7   **Running and Maintaining the Database** **103**

Where Are the Databases? 104

Using OpenBaseManager 105

    Starting and Stopping Databases 106

    Using the Toolbar 106

Configuring the Database 107

OpenBase Preferences 108

    Basic Preferences 108

    NetworkPreferences 108

    Host Password 110

    License Preferences 110

Backing Up Databases 110

Restoring from Backups 113

Importing from Spreadsheets 114

Replicating Databases 114

Part III   **Interacting with Databases Using Enterprise Objects**

Chapter 8   **Introduction to Enterprise Objects Framework** **119**

Databases, Objects, and Enterprise Objects Framework 121

Factoring Applications and Data 122

Factoring Logic and Data 123
Design Strategies: Which End to Start From 124
How Enterprise Objects Framework
Works with WebObjects 125
Using Enterprise Objects 125
The Enterprise Objects Framework Structure 126

Chapter 9 **Enterprise Objects Framework Design Issues** **129**
The WebObjects Application 130
Start Page 131
Entry Page 132
Creating the Page in WebObjects Builder 132
Writing the Code in Project Builder 135
Search Page 138
Creating the Page in WebObjects Builder 138
Writing the Code in Project Builder 139
Summary Display Page 142
Creating the Page in WebObjects Builder 142
Writing the Code in Project Builder 145

Chapter 10 **Persistent Objects** **147**
Issues of Persistence 148
Faulting 149
Batch Faulting 150
Prefetching 150
Fetching Data with an Editing Context 151
Getting the Editing Context 151
Building the Query 152
Fetching the Data 153
Fetching Data with a Display Group 153
Declare the Display Group 154
Place a Display Group in a WORepetition 154
Create a Fetch Spec 156

Chapter 11 **Using EOModeler** **161**
Getting Started with EOModeler 162
Creating a Model Automatically from OpenBase Tables 164
Setting Up the Model 164
Editing the Model 168
Creating Java Classes for Your Model Entities 170
Creating Database Tables from Your Model 171

Chapter 12 **Working with the Model and the Database** **179**
Creating Java Classes from EOModeler 180

Using EOGenericRecord 183
    A Walk-Through of the Default Implementation 183
    Instantiating an Enterprise Objects Framework Object 186
EOEnterpriseObject 188
    Extra Processing 188
    Validation 188

Part IV	**Creating Dynamic Web Sites with WebObjects**

Chapter 13	**WebObjects at Work** **193**

Looking at a WebObjects Site 194
    The Home Page 195
    Static Pages: Privacy Statement 196
    Form Submission Pages for Data Entry 196
    Static Response Pages 196
    Dynamic Response Pages 198
    Form Submission Pages for Searching 198
    Search Response Page 199
    Other Pages on the Site 200
What Happens 200
    ConfirmAddEdit 203
    AddDiscussion 208
    AddDiscussion.wod 210
How It Happens 211
    Adaptors 211
    State Management 211
    Request-Response Loop 213

Chapter 14	**Using WebObjects Builder** **215**

Using WebObjects Builder 216
    Window Controls 217
    Text and Image Editing Controls 219
    HTML Controls 219
    WebObject Element Controls 220
Binding Keys and Actions to Properties 222
    Binding Attributes with Text 222
    Binding Attributes Graphically 225
Creating New Bindings 227

Chapter 15	**Using Project Builder** **229**

Creating Projects 230
Editing Projects 232
Editing Components 234

Creating a Simple Component 234
Creating a Display Group Component 236
Building and Launching WebObjects Applications 240

Chapter 16   Using Dynamic Elements **243**

How Dynamic Elements Work 244
What Dynamic Elements Do (Methods) 244
What Dynamic Elements Know (Properties) 245
How It Works 245
Syntax for WebObjects Dynamic Elements 246
Programming Support for Dynamic Elements 247
HTML Elements 247
FORM Elements 254
Programming Elements 263

Chapter 17   Implementing the Request-Response Loop **271**

Classes that Implement the Request-Reponse Loop 272
WOElement 272
WOMessage 273
WOContext 276
WORequest 276
WOResponse 277
The Request-Response Cycle in Action 277
takeValuesFromRequest 278
invokeActionForRequest 279
appendToResponse 279

Chapter 18   Using Direct and Component Actions **281**

WebObjects URLs 283
Using WebObjects in a cgi-bin or Server Directory 283
Using WebObjects in API Mode 285
Why This Matters 285
WOApplication 286
Using Multiple WOApplication Instances 287
The Role of WOApplication 287
WOAdaptor 288
WORequestHandler 289
WOComponent and Component Actions 290
WODirectAction and Direct Actions 291

Chapter 19   State and Session Management **293**

Identity, State, Persistence, and
Transactions: An Introduction 294
Examples of State 295

Identity 296

State 298

Persistence 299

Transactions 300

Where State Happens 301

URL and Form-Based State 301

Browser State 302

Client State 304

WebObjects State 304

Database State 305

Server State 305

Intermediate State 306

Designing for State 306

Identifying Your Needs 306

Improving Your Design 307

Using Sessions Effectively 308

Storing and Retrieving Session Data 308

Setting Timeouts 310

Controlling the WebObjects (Server) Cache 311

Controlling the Browser (Client) Cache 312

Storing State Explicitly 312

Awake/Sleep Opportunities 313

Session Stores 313

Chapter 20   XML and WebObjects **315**

XML Basics 316

XML Element Formatting 317

XML Element Names and Attributes 318

XML vs. HTML 318

The Document Object Model 319

Why Use XML? 319

Using XML with WebObjects 320

XML and Messages 320

XML and Data 321

Chapter 21   Advanced WebObjects Topics **335**

Debugging Tips and Tools 336

Logs 337

Monitor 337

Warning Messages 337

Code Reviews 337

Stress Testing 338

Normal Operation Metrics 338

Database Performance 338
   Batch Faulting 339
   Prefetching 339
   Caching 339
   SQL logs 340
   Database Load 340
Handling Errors 340
   Customizing the Default Error Page 341
   Implementing Your Own Error Page 341

Part V   **Jump-Starting WebObjects and OpenBase**

Chapter 22   **Direct to Web** **347**
What Is Direct to Web? 348
Creating a Direct to Web Project 349
Direct to Web Looks 353
   Basic Look 353
   Plain Look 354
   WebObjects Look 355
   Other Direct to Web Pages 358
Customizing Direct to Web 359
   Using WebObjects Builder and Project Builder 359
Using WebAssistant 360
Using Direct to Web in Other WebObjects Applications 366
   Linking to Direct to Web 366
   Using the Direct to Web Frameworks 367

Chapter 23   **Java Client** **369**
What Is a WebObjects Java Client? 370
Direct to Java Client 374
Creating a Java Client Project 374
Writing Java Client Applications 376
Running a Java Client 382
   Do Not Launch a Web Browser 382
   Run the Java Client Application from Terminal 383

Chapter 24   **Reusable Components in WebObjects** **387**
Using the Palette 388
WOExtensions Palette 389
   WOAnyField 389
   WOAppleScript 390
   WOBatchNavigationBar 390
   WOCheckboxMatrix, WORadioButtonMatrix, and WOTable 390
   WOCollapsibleComponentContent 390

WOCompletionBar 391

WODictionaryRepetition 391

WOMetaRefresh 391

WOSimpleArrayDisplay and WOSimpleArrayDisplay2 391

WOSortOrder and WOSortOrderManyKey 392

WOTabPanel 392

Premade Elements Palette 392

Direct to Web Palette 393

JavaScript Palette 394

JavaClient Palette 395

WOSMIL Palette 396

Creating a New Palette 397

Creating Reusable WebObjects Component Objects 398

Chapter 25   **Reusable Databases and Frameworks in OpenBase and WebObjects** . . .   **403**

Frameworks in WebObjects 404

Implementing a Framework 405

Using a Framework 406

Example Frameworks in WebObjects 406

Reusing Databases 407

Duplicating Databases 407

Partitions 407

Reusing Data 408

Reusing Database Designs and Schemas 408

Data Mining, Warehousing, and Analysis 409

Reusing Models 410

Reuse Considerations 410

Part VI   **Deployment Issues**

Chapter 26   **Running a Database on a Network** **415**

Preparing for Deployment 416

Moving the Database to Production 417

Location: Where Is the Database? 419

Colocation and Data Centers 419

Outsourcing 420

Hosting 420

Environments 421

Time: Keeping It Running 421

Maintaining Uptime 421

Planning Maintenance 423

Planning Backups 423

Issues for Small-Scale Networks 423

Acknowledgments

Many people have contributed to the development and production of this book. In more or less chronological order, they are listed here.

To begin with, Carole McClendon at Waterside Productions worked her usual magic with the initial proposal and contract. At McGraw-Hill/Osborne, Jane Brownlow and her assistants Emma Acker and Ross Doll helped move the project along. Senior project editors Carolyn Welch and Lisa Theobald provided excellent assistance in making the book look like it does. Copy editors Bob Campbell and Chrisa Hotchkiss helped to make the text clearer and consistent. Finally, Lydia Griffey and Sherry Bonelli helped see the book through its debut into the world.

In addition, Scott Keith of OpenBase International was a great source of information not only about OpenBase but also about WebObjects. His technical review of the book is a significant contribution.

Notwithstanding the help of so many people, any errors are the sole handiwork of the author.

Preface

The history of the computer age has been of large, complicated devices and technologies becoming smaller and easier to use. This is as true of computers themselves as of the software that runs on them.

When WebObjects was created, it was a tool for the largest corporations to use. Their support staffs included people who were experts in database administration, telecommunications, and programming. Today, WebObjects is a tool for use in small to medium size businesses as well as in enterprises of global scale. That change has come about in large part because of the rapidly increasing demands of small to medium size businesses for dynamic Web sites, sophisticated data management, and transaction processing. The level of sophistication of users has dramatically increased—both Web site developers who use WebObjects to build their sites and end users who use the WebObjects applications.

WebObjects may be the easiest application development tool for the complex applications expected today in all but the most trivial Web sites. Its Direct to Web and Direct to Java Client tools are unsurpassed for building applications and even ad hoc projects for single user, one-time use.

However, WebObjects does pose a problem for many people. Since it brings together so many disciplines and technologies, the learning curve can be steep. This book attempts to address that issue. It provides the background of the various technologies involved, and it shows you how to work with them to achieve your goals. The focus is on real-world problems. You will find actual code sprinkled throughout the book, and you will find the code repeated in several sections.

As one example, the concept of WebObjects display groups is covered twice. Display groups let you specify data to be retrieved from a database and then to display it using the typical Web format of batches of records. If you want, you can add links to each of the entries so that people can explore further (or add items to a shopping cart). You will find display groups discussed in Part III, which focuses on the database side of things with Enterprise Objects Framework. Then, you will find it addressed again in Part IV, which focuses on WebObjects itself.

WebObjects applications almost always use relational databases for their data management. A variety of such databases are used. In this book, OpenBase is used to demonstrate database issues. You can download a free evaluation copy of OpenBase from their Web site (http://www.openbase.com). OpenBase works particularly well with WebObjects, but you will find that any relational database can be integrated with WebObjects. Furthermore, the tools that OpenBase provides are similar to those provided with other databases. The lingua franca of modern relational databases, SQL, is what makes it all work.

How This Book Is Organized

There are six parts to this book.

Welcome to WebObjects and OpenBase

The first part of the book gets you started with the basic concepts behind WebObjects including application servers, object-oriented programming, and modern database technology. If you are experienced with programming, you may be familiar with some of these concepts. Pay particular attention to Chapter 2, The World of Application Servers. This is the fundamental architecture of WebObjects, and everything that follows relies on these principles.

Building a Database with OpenBase

Almost all WebObjects applications use relational databases, and this part of the book introduces you to the concepts and shows you how to use OpenBase to create and manage databases. (Other databases work in much the same way, so this section is applicable to them, too.)

If you are used to desktop databases or to single-user applications, some of the concepts here may be new to you. In particular, whereas personal productivity tools and databases combine interface and database, database managers such as OpenBase separate the two.

Interacting with Databases Using Enterprise Objects Framework

Enterprise Objects Framework converts the relational database you use into objects that can be used in the object-oriented world of WebObjects. This is actually one of the most exciting aspects of WebObjects; it addresses an issue that developers have